I0813870

CORE LIBRARY OF US STATES

WASHINGTON

BY HANNAH PERKINS

CONTENT CONSULTANT
Chris Friday, PhD
Professor, College of Humanities & Social Sciences
Western Washington University

Core Library
An Imprint of Abdo Publishing
abdobooks.com

Published by Abdo Publishing, a division of ABDO, PO Box 398166, Minneapolis, Minnesota 55439.

Printed in the United States of America, North Mankato, Minnesota.
052022
092022

Cover Photo: Shutterstock Images
Interior Photos: Sean Pavone/Shutterstock Images, 4–5, 45; Red Line Editorial, 8 (Washington) , 8 (USA); MPI/Archive Photos/Getty Images, 10–11; Everett Collection/Shutterstock Images, 13; GG Digital Arts/Shutterstock Images, 17 (flag); Shutterstock Images, 17 (bird), 17 (orca), 25, 27, 39; Thomas Hagenau/Shutterstock Images, 17 (flower); Abbie Warnock-Matthews/Shutterstock Images, 17 (tree); Galyna Andrushko/Shutterstock Images, 20–21; Brian Schlittenhardt/Shutterstock Images, 23, 43; David Ryder/Bloomberg/Getty Images, 28–29; First Class Photography/Shutterstock Images, 31; Earl's Photos/Shutterstock Images, 34–35; Ted S. Warren/AP Images, 37

Editor: Arnold Ringstad
Series Designer: Joshua Olson

Library of Congress Control Number: 2021951571

Publisher's Cataloging-in-Publication Data

Names: Perkins, Hannah, author.
Title: Washington / by Hannah Perkins
Description: Minneapolis, Minnesota : Abdo Publishing, 2023 | Series: Core library of US states | Includes online resources and index.
Identifiers: ISBN 9781532197895 (lib. bdg.) | ISBN 9781098270650 (ebook)
Subjects: LCSH: U.S. states--Juvenile literature. | Western States (U.S.)--Juvenile literature. | Washington (State)--History--Juvenile literature. | Physical geography--United States--Juvenile literature.
Classification: DDC 979.7--dc23

Population demographics broken down by race and ethnicity come from the 2019 census estimate. Population totals come from the 2020 census.

CONTENTS

CHAPTER ONE

THE EVERGREEN STATE

Light rain starts to fall as tourists gather near the Space Needle, the most famous landmark in Seattle, Washington. The cloudy weather is no surprise. Seattle gets rain about 150 days each year. The tourists hope that clouds won't ruin the view from 605 feet (184 m) above the city.

The Space Needle opened in 1962. It was part of the World's Fair that Seattle hosted that year. The towering structure's modern look represented the new frontier of

The Space Needle is a world-famous symbol of Seattle, Washington.

EVERGREEN INDEED

More than half of Washington's land area is forested. This adds up to about 22 million acres (9 million ha) of trees. The federal government manages about 43 percent of these forests. This includes national parks and other recreation areas. Washington State oversees 12 percent of its forests. About 7 percent of the forests belong to American Indian peoples. More than 21 percent is managed by companies that produce wood and paper products.

space exploration. The Space Needle is still a symbol of innovation. Seattle is now known as a technology center. Companies such as Microsoft and Amazon have major offices in the area.

As the tourists ride the elevator to the top of the Space Needle, they see the sun peek out from behind the passing clouds. The brighter weather lets them enjoy the 360-degree view at the top. Across Puget Sound they can see Mount Rainier, the Cascades, and the Olympic Mountains. These tree-covered mountains gave Washington its nickname, the Evergreen State.

WHERE IS WASHINGTON?

Washington is in the Pacific Northwest. This region is in the northwestern corner of the United States. Washington is bordered by two other states. Idaho lies to the east, and Oregon is to the south. The Pacific Ocean is on Washington's western coast. British Columbia, Canada, is to the north.

The Salish Sea extends into Washington. It is protected on both sides by land. The sea includes other bodies of water, such as Puget Sound. Historically, boat travel made cities on the sound easy to reach. Today some of the state's biggest cities are located there.

Seattle has long been an important city for trade and shipping. It is now known for technology companies, medical sciences, and tourism. Washington has several other important cities. The capital city is Olympia, located in western Washington. Other large western cities include Tacoma and Vancouver. Eastern cities include Spokane and Walla Walla.

MAP OF WASHINGTON

Washington has a long coastline, tall mountains, and large inland areas. How do you think life in these regions might differ?

The Cascade Mountains divide the state. Many peaks in the Cascades and the Olympic Mountains have glaciers. These masses of ice feed into the state's major rivers. Long important for food and transportation, today these rivers are also used for recreation and to generate electricity. From bustling modern cities to thrilling outdoor adventures, Washington offers something for everyone.

PERSPECTIVES

THE ORIGINAL VANCOUVER

Founded as Fort Vancouver in 1825, Vancouver is Washington's fourth-largest city. People visit it for a huge farmer's market, many biking trails, and outdoor concerts in the summer. But some people from outside the area confuse Vancouver with a city of the same name in British Columbia, Canada. That city was established in 1886. Freelance writer Kristin Norton explains, "Locals differentiate the cities by referring to their city as Vancouver USA and the Canadian city as Vancouver BC for the many (many) people from out of the area who ask, 'Isn't that in Canada?'"

CHAPTER TWO

HISTORY OF WASHINGTON

People have lived in the Washington area for more than 10,000 years. The ancient peoples of Washington spoke many languages and formed many tribes. However, researchers sometimes divide them into two major groups. Coast Salish Indians lived west of the Cascades. Columbia River Plateau Indians lived in inland areas.

The Marmes Rock Shelter is a natural cave along the Snake River. Archaeologists have found artifacts there that date back about

American Indian people in Washington historically used long poles to catch salmon. Some Native fishers continue this tradition today.

10,000 years. They believe that Plateau peoples lived there. Ancestors of today's American Indian peoples lived in the area when glaciers covered parts of northern Washington. They fished for salmon and hunted whales and other animals. Some also collected berries and shellfish. Specific ways of life varied from region to region.

EUROPEAN SETTLEMENT

In the late 1700s, European traders came to the Washington coast. They traded with American Indian nations. These early Europeans were looking for seals. Seal fur was valuable for clothing. The fur trade later shifted to beavers.

In 1803 President Thomas Jefferson bought a large area of land for the United States. This was the Louisiana Purchase. The land stretched across much of the western part of the continent. Jefferson asked Meriwether Lewis and William Clark to explore this region. Lewis and Clark set off in 1804 from Missouri.

An artist's depiction shows Lewis and Clark along the Columbia River.

They arrived in Washington in 1805 and continued all the way to the Pacific Ocean. This land was not part of the Louisiana Purchase. When the group arrived in Washington, the Nimiipuu greeted them as allies and traders. The explorers' relations with other tribes, such as the Chinook, were not as peaceful.

Early traders established strong relationships with the region's American Indians. But things began to shift by the 1840s. Diseases swept through Indian communities, and American settlers began to arrive. By the 1850s, thousands of settlers arrived each year. The US government negotiated treaties for the land.

SEATTLE'S NAMESAKE

The city of Seattle was named after Chief Si'ahl. He was a leader of the Duwamish people. Si'ahl lived in the mid-1800s. He welcomed white settlers. Si'ahl and the Duwamish people helped the newcomers survive in the area. They taught the settlers how to find food and build strong shelters. Descendants of the Duwamish are members of many of the tribes that live near Puget Sound today.

These treaties created reservations. It took several years for the reservations to actually be established. Not all American Indians moved to these reservations. Those who did generally continued their normal ways of life for the rest of the 1800s.

BECOMING A US STATE

In the early 1800s, the United States and Great Britain both occupied the region known as the Oregon Country. Both nations wanted their traders to work in this area. By the 1840s, the fur trade was declining, and settlers were moving in.

In 1846 the two countries agreed to divide the region. The northern part fell under British control. The southern part belonged to the United States. Two years later, the United States established the Oregon Territory there.

The Oregon Territory covered a huge area. It was tough to manage. The territorial government oversaw settlers and managed relationships with American Indians. In 1853 the US government carved out the Washington Territory from this land. It included present-day Washington State and parts of what are now Idaho and Montana. In 1863 the Idaho Territory was created. By this time, most of Washington's modern borders were in place.

Reaching Washington became easier in 1883. The Northern Pacific Railway connected the Midwest to Washington. Trains ran from Minnesota all the way to Seattle and Puget Sound. Trains brought trade goods to the state's ports. Washington became the

PERSPECTIVES

THE VIEW OF SEATTLE

American author Elia Peattie traveled by railroad to visit Seattle in the fall of 1889. She wrote about her impressions in a travel guide published the following year. She was especially struck by Seattle's beauty. "The shining peaks of Mounts [Rainier], Baker, Adams, and St. Helens pierced the bright sky," she wrote. "I concluded that this was a city any man might be proud to live in."

forty-second state on November 11, 1889.

Seattle was booming in this period. Its businesses and industries brought workers from around the world. Asian migrants came to Washington. They worked for railroads, salmon canneries, and lumber camps. Some stayed, and their descendants still live in the state today. Black Americans also settled in Washington, working for railroads and in cities.

BUILDING MODERN WASHINGTON

In the 1930s the government began building huge dams in Washington. These included the Bonneville

WASHINGTON

QUICK FACTS

Washington has many things that make it unique. Which of the state's symbols would you most like to see in person?

Abbreviation: WA
Nickname: The Evergreen State
Motto: *Alki* (Chinook word meaning "By and by")
Date of statehood: November 11, 1889
Capital: Olympia
Population: 7,705,281
Area: 71,298 square miles (184,661 sq km)

STATE SYMBOLS

State bird
Willow goldfinch

State marine mammal
Orca

State flower
Coast rhododendron

State tree
Western hemlock

Dam in 1937 and the Grand Coulee Dam in 1941. These dams helped control flooding. Their hydroelectric plants generated electricity. But the dams also created problems. They blocked salmon migration and flooded American Indian fishing areas. Tribes continue to protest the loss of these fishing rights.

During World War II (1939–1945), Boeing built thousands of airplanes for the US military. The company helped make Washington a center of technology. Technology remains important in Washington today. The mix of advanced technology and amazing natural beauty draws many people to Washington. It is one of the fastest-growing US states.

GOVERNMENT

Washington's government has three branches. Each has different responsibilities. The legislative branch writes and votes on proposed laws, called bills. The executive branch includes the governor, who has the power to sign bills into law. The last branch is the judicial branch, made up of the state's courts.

Washington also has 29 federally recognized American Indian tribes. Each of these tribes has its own constitution and system of government. These tribal governments are separate from Washington's state government. The tribes and the state work together on issues such as salmon harvests, certain taxes, and gambling.

FURTHER EVIDENCE

Chapter Two discusses Lewis and Clark's famous expedition from Missouri to the Pacific Ocean. What was one of the main points of this part of the chapter? What evidence is included to support this point? Read the article at the website below. Does the information on the website support this point? Does it present new evidence?

LEWIS AND CLARK IN WASHINGTON

abdocorelibrary.com/washington

CHAPTER THREE

GEOGRAPHY AND CLIMATE

Washington has a variety of landforms, including both mountains and plains. The Olympic Mountains are near the Pacific Ocean. A valley separates the Olympic and Cascade Mountains. Beyond the Cascades is the Columbia Basin. This area has rocky ridges and plateaus as well as river canyons.

Volcanoes created many of the state's landforms. Several peaks on the Cascade Range are volcanic cones. Some of these

Washington has a diverse mix of waterways, forests, rocky landscapes, and more.

PERSPECTIVES

MOUNT SAINT HELENS ERUPTION

One of the most famous peaks in Washington's Cascade Range is the Mount Saint Helens volcano. Its eruption in 1980 was the deadliest in US history. It killed 57 people and caused more than $1 billion in damage. Barbara Webster was leaving the state on an airplane when it began. She said, "The pilot flew right over the top and we looked down into the eruption. . . . He must have gotten word from the airport to get out of there because he made what felt like a 90-degree turn."

volcanoes are still active. They could erupt again. The Columbia Basin is made up of basalt, a volcanic rock.

NATURAL DISASTERS AND WEATHER

Washington's location and volcanoes put the state at risk for several kinds of natural disasters. Washington's coast is near where two tectonic plates meet. Movement of these plates can cause earthquakes. It may also trigger volcanic eruptions.

Washington is known for being rainy. Heavy rainfall can cause landslides in hilly regions. But only the

The aftermath of the 1980 eruption of Mount Saint Helens can still be seen today.

western region gets a lot of rain. The eastern part of the state is much drier due to the Cascade Range. The tall mountains often block rain clouds from the west. This effect is known as a rain shadow.

The western and coastal parts of the state are rainy and have relatively few temperature changes during the year. The weather is often mild. Winters and summers have similar temperatures. In contrast, eastern Washington has hot summers. Its winters are also colder.

PLANTS AND ANIMALS

Diverse plants and animals live throughout Washington. Much of the state is forested. However, different regions have different types of trees. In the eastern mountains, juniper, western larch, and ponderosa pine trees grow. The mountains are also home to mountain goats. Forests closer to the coast feature western hemlocks and red cedars. Eagles fly high above the forests and beaches. The state flower is the coast rhododendron. It grows west of the Cascades. The state bird, the willow goldfinch, lives throughout the state.

The Hoh Rain Forest covers large areas of land. This temperate rain forest experiences mild temperatures and plenty of rainfall. Elk, black bears, and otters are all

Walking paths give visitors a chance to explore the Hoh Rain Forest.

found here. The rain forest is also important because it traps carbon dioxide. Carbon dioxide is one of the gases that causes climate change.

THE COLUMBIA RIVER AND ITS FISH

The Columbia River begins in Canada, then flows through eastern Washington. It forms the state's southern border with Oregon. The river empties into the Pacific Ocean. The Columbia has many types of fish, including the state fish, the steelhead trout.

Another important fish is salmon. For thousands of years, American Indians relied on these fish. Ocean animals, including seals and orcas, also eat salmon. But overfishing, dam construction, and the growth of cities have hurt salmon populations. Salmon travel up rivers such as the Columbia River each year to breed. Dams along the way make it difficult to reach the breeding grounds. Fourteen types of salmon are at risk of dying out in Washington. Washington's Department of Natural Resources works with tribal leaders throughout the state. They are hoping to restore salmon populations to healthier levels.

ORCAS

Orcas are Washington's state marine mammal. These black-and-white sea animals are also known as killer whales. Orcas eat seals and fish. They hunt for food in groups called pods. Orcas are fierce predators. But they are endangered. Overfishing reduces the amount of prey for orcas. People are working to protect orca pods along the Pacific Coast. Tribes such as the Lummi Nation and Samish Indian Nation have adopted and named specific orcas in an effort to protect them.

Beyond the river, the Columbia Basin is drier. The plains are filled with tall grasses and sagebrush. Sagebrush is part of

Trout are an important part of Washington's history, culture, and economy.

the habitat for the threatened sage grouse. As plains and sagebrush disappear because of development, habitat for this bird also disappears.

EXPLORE ONLINE

Chapter Three discusses Washington's climate and geography. The website below focuses on the same topics. As you know, every source is different. How is the information at the website different from the information in this chapter? What information is the same? What information did you learn from the website?

WASHINGTON'S DIVERSE CLIMATE AND GEOGRAPHY

abdocorelibrary.com/washington

CHAPTER FOUR

RESOURCES AND ECONOMY

Many of Washington's biggest companies are in Seattle. Companies such as Amazon, Microsoft, and Nintendo have offices in the city. Washington once relied on agriculture, forests, and fishing. These industries are still important today. Eastern Washington is a major producer of winter wheat. Farms across the state grow crops such as potatoes, lentils, apples, cranberries, and pears.

Starbucks, which is based in Washington, runs a combination café and coffee bean roastery in Seattle.

Coffee beans do not grow in Washington. But coffee shops do. Starbucks opened its first coffee shop in Seattle in 1971. By 2020 the company had more than 30,000 locations around the world and employed 349,000 people. Washington is also known for having many local coffee shops.

PERSPECTIVES

WHAT MADE STARBUCKS SO SUCCESSFUL?

Starbucks makes more than $22 billion each year. What led to this huge success? Business experts point out that the company filled a hole in the coffee industry. Analyst Liraz Margalit explained that before Starbucks, most people drank coffee either at home or at work. Now they had another place to sit and enjoy the beverage. She said, "Starbucks doesn't compete with other coffee houses, it competes with going to see a movie."

AIRCRAFT AND SPACECRAFT

The growth of industry in the 1900s caused many people to move from rural areas to big cities. One industry that grew in Seattle was aircraft building. The Boeing Company was founded

Workers build airliners in huge Boeing factories in Washington.

in Seattle in 1916. Most Boeing planes are still made near Seattle.

The state is also home to space companies. SpaceX has several offices in the city. This company works on building spacecraft and rockets. More than three dozen

BOEING

William Boeing founded Pacific Aero Products in 1916. The next year, the company was renamed the Boeing Airplane Company. In 1966 Boeing built an airplane factory in Everett, Washington. It includes the largest building in the world by volume. Today workers there build the advanced Boeing 787 airliner.

smaller space-related companies also operate in Washington. Together they employ more than 6,200 people in the state.

RENEWABLE ENERGY

Washington has a mix of renewable energy resources. The most important is water. Rivers such as the Columbia provide hydroelectricity. In 2019 hydroelectric plants generated 62 percent of Washington's electricity.

The second-biggest renewable energy resource in Washington is wind. More than 1,700 turbines in the state turn wind into electricity. The largest wind farm is located in southeastern Washington along the Snake River.

STRAIGHT TO THE SOURCE

Terry Flores is the executive director of Northwest River Partners. She explains how the dams help businesses as well as the environment:

The federal dams, in addition to generating power, have a series of locks that are key to Washington's export trade, providing vital navigation for barges through the Columbia-Snake river system, a 465-mile [748-km] river highway connecting farmers and businesses to markets across the region and the world. Ten percent—or 4.2 million tons [3.8 million metric tons]—of all Northwest exports pass through the four Snake dams by barge each year. This "river of commerce" moves grain, fertilizers, potatoes, wood products and other commodities faster than by train or truck—and with far less fuel and carbon emissions.

Source: Terry Flores. "Washington's Best-Kept Renewable Secret: Hydropower." *Seattle Business*, n.d., seattlebusinessmag.com. Accessed 14 Sept. 2021.

BACK IT UP

The author of this passage is using evidence to support a point. Write a paragraph describing the point the author is making and list two pieces of evidence the author provides.

CHAPTER FIVE

PEOPLE AND PLACES

About 7.7 million people live in Washington. More than 67 percent of the state's population consists of white people who are not Hispanic or Latino. About 13 percent are Hispanic or Latino, nearly 10 percent are Asian, and more than 4 percent are Black. Washington also has a larger American Indian population than most other US states have. More than 140,000 American Indians make up around 2 percent of the state's population.

Mount Rainier is visible from Tacoma, one of Washington's largest cities.

Many people live in the Seattle-Tacoma-Bellevue area. These three cities are on Puget Sound. This is also where many of the state's businesses are located. More than half of Washington's people live in this area. Seattle and its surrounding cities have a high cost of living. Finding affordable housing can be difficult.

FAMOUS WASHINGTONIANS

Many famous people began their lives in Washington. Microsoft cofounder Bill Gates was born in Seattle. The tech billionaire has an estate in his hometown that is almost as big as the White House.

Billy Frank Jr. was a Nisqually leader who fought for the rights of American Indians. An 1845 treaty gave American Indians fishing rights. But the state tried to take away these rights. Frank led fish-ins, protests in which American Indians fished in their traditional lands. Washington police arrested many people during the fish-ins. The issue eventually made it to the federal court system in 1970. Frank was one of 49 people who

Billy Frank Jr.'s activism brought about important change on the issue of fishing rights.

spoke to the court. The court ruled in favor of Frank and the others. Frank died in 2014. The next year, he was honored with the Presidential Medal of Freedom.

Other Washington residents became stars of sports and entertainment. Olympic speed skating champion Apolo Ohno hails from Washington. Basketball star Nate Robinson was born in Seattle. Actress Anna Faris grew up in the state and attended the University of Washington.

Washington has had a large influence on music culture. Famed guitarist Jimi Hendrix was born in Seattle. Grunge bands Nirvana, Pearl Jam, and

PERSPECTIVES

MAKING A DIFFERENCE

After the United States went to war with Japan in 1941, the US government imprisoned many Japanese Americans in camps. Alan Sugiyama's mother was imprisoned in one of these camps. As a young person, he committed his life to fighting for racial justice. In 1989 Sugiyama became the first Asian American elected to the Seattle School Board. Although he died in 2017, his legacy lives on. In 2020 Seattle renamed one of its schools Alan T. Sugiyama High School at South Lake. The school's website calls his life "an enduring example to students of how one person's actions and determination can break down barriers to racial and educational equity."

Soundgarden were also products of Seattle. Musicians Kenny Loggins and Ben Gibbard are both from Washington too.

THINGS TO DO IN WASHINGTON

Washington has many things to see and do. Sports fans can attend professional baseball, basketball, football, soccer, and even rugby games. Art lovers can see Chihuly Garden and Glass. Dale Chihuly is an artist who specializes in

Pike Place Market, which first opened in 1907, is a popular destination in downtown Seattle.

glass blowing. Downtown Seattle includes the famous Pike Place Market and the Seattle Aquarium.

Washington has many museums where people can learn about the state's history and cultures. The Washington State History Museum in Tacoma is filled with interactive exhibits about Washington's past. The Northwest Museum of Arts and Culture in Spokane is the largest museum celebrating the northwest region. The Hibulb Cultural Center and Natural History Preserve

NATIONAL PARKS

Washington is home to three national parks. Mount Rainier National Park features meadows, lakes, and the giant peak for which the park was named. Located on the northwest coastline, Olympic National Park has several beaches. North Cascades National Park can be reached in two ways. Visitors can drive up North Cascades Scenic Byway or ride on the Lady of the Lake Ferry across Lake Chelan.

focuses on the cultures of the Tulalip peoples. The Omak Stampede Indian Encampment and Pow-wow also celebrates American Indian cultures.

The state boasts many outdoor activities. The Pacific Crest Trail spans from Canada to Mexico. More than 500 miles (800 km) of the mountainous trail are in Washington. The Summit at Snoqualmie is a popular ski resort. National and state parks in Washington feature mountains, forests, and rivers. People look for orcas on Puget Sound or kayak along the coasts and waterways. From big cities to big forests, Washington has many places to explore.

STRAIGHT TO THE SOURCE

Soccer superstar Megan Rapinoe and her partner, WNBA player Sue Bird, live in Seattle's Queen Anne neighborhood. When asked what she likes best about the city, Rapinoe replied:

> *When I first came to Seattle to play, it was in the summer months. I lived with a close friend and teammate, Stephanie Cox, who lives in Gig Harbor. My initial thoughts were just how breathtaking this city is. I loved being surrounded by nature and water but still having the city right there. I think my impressions are the same: Seattle is absolutely beautiful. . . . I love coffee, so I am very spoiled here. One of my favorite things is to go out on Lake Washington. I have some friends with boats, and there is nothing better than [spending time] on the boat with the sun shining.*

Source: Megan Rapinoe. "Seattle Ambassador: Megan Rapinoe." *Visit Seattle*, 2021, visitseattle.org. Accessed 14 Sept. 2021.

WHAT'S THE BIG IDEA?

Take a close look at Rapinoe's words. What is her main idea? What evidence is used to support her point? Come up with a few sentences showing how Rapinoe uses two or three pieces of evidence to support her main point.

IMPORTANT DATES

About 10,000 years ago
Plateau peoples live in Marmes Rock Shelter.

1700s CE
Coastal peoples trade with European fur traders.

1805
Nimiipuu people help Lewis and Clark when the explorers reach Washington.

1840s
Large numbers of American settlers move to Washington.

1883
The Northern Pacific Railway connects Washington with big cities in the Midwest.

1889
Washington becomes a state on November 11.

1916
William Boeing establishes his airplane company.

1962
The Space Needle opens for the World's Fair.

1971
Starbucks opens its first location in Seattle.

1980
Mount Saint Helens erupts.

1990s
Technology companies spur major growth in the Seattle area.

STOP AND THINK

Tell the Tale

Chapter One discusses a trip to the Space Needle. Imagine that you are taking a ride to the top of this famous structure. Write 200 words about your experience. Describe what you see and hear, as well as how you feel standing at the top.

Surprise Me

This book discusses the state of Washington. After reading this book, what two or three facts about Washington did you find most surprising? Write a few sentences about each fact. Why did you find each fact surprising?

Say What?

Studying a state can mean learning a lot of new vocabulary. Find five words in this book you've never seen before. Use a dictionary to find out what they mean. Then write the meanings in your own words and use each word in a new sentence.

Dig Deeper

After reading this book, what questions do you still have about Washington? With an adult's help, find a few reliable sources that can help you answer your questions. Write a paragraph about what you learned.

GLOSSARY

climate change
a human-caused global crisis involving long-term changes in Earth's temperature and weather patterns

culture
the way a group of people lives; its customs, beliefs, and laws

endangered
at risk of dying out

hydroelectricity
electricity that is created by moving water

innovation
a new idea, method, or device

pod
a group of orcas or dolphins

reservation
an area of land set aside for American Indian people

tectonic plates
massive pieces of rock that make up Earth's crust

temperate
a climate that does not have extremely hot or cold temperatures

treaty
an official agreement between governments

ONLINE RESOURCES

To learn more about Washington, visit our free resource websites below.

Visit **abdocorelibrary.com** or scan this QR code for free Common Core resources for teachers and students, including vetted activities, multimedia, and booklinks, for deeper subject comprehension.

Visit **abdobooklinks.com** or scan this QR code for free additional online weblinks for further learning. These links are routinely monitored and updated to provide the most current information available.

LEARN MORE

Conley, Kate. *Engineering the Space Needle*. Abdo, 2018.

Johnson, Anna Maria. *Washington*. Cavendish Square, 2020.

INDEX

About the Author

Hannah Perkins is an author of children's books who lives in Maine.